Blend Hunt

Set 4

Written by Kassi Gilmour

Practise the sounds

m s t a p i f c r o d h e n
g k ck u l ll ss ff b j w wh y
th sh v qu z zz x

The Blend Hunt books are designed to help children practise blending new sounds within each set. Once each word is successfully blended, children search for the item that matches the words they have read on each page.

Practise tricky words

he she to do me we was
you no go they of are
have all her day for like

Blend Hunt
Set 4

Written by Kassi Gilmour

six ducks
shells

soft cubs

rush

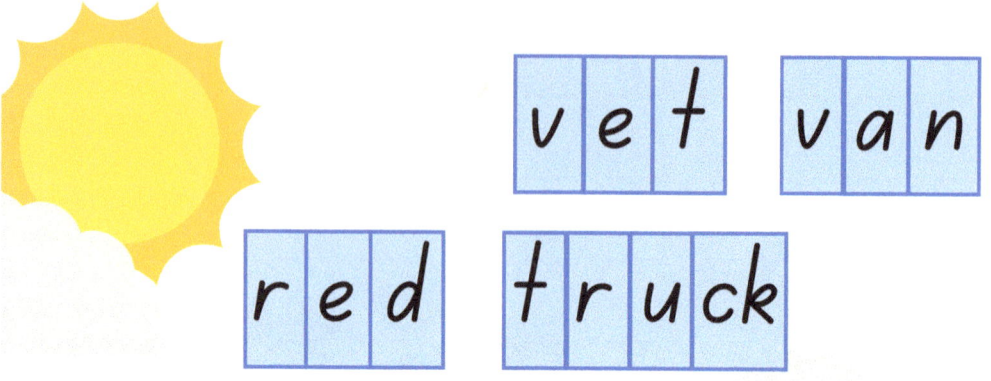

vet van

red truck

stick leg

clock

forest   stroll

splash vest

buzz

quick rabbit

foxes

black lamp

shelf

zip lock bags

pic/nic

parrot   lamp

black flag

Sound Wall

These graphemes are introduced in Set 4. The images are provided to support sound recognition and help children remember each phoneme.

Gold

Written by Kassi Gilmour

Practise the sounds

m s t a p i f c r o d h e n
g k ck u l ll ss ff b j w wh y
th sh v qu z zz x

Practise blending sounds

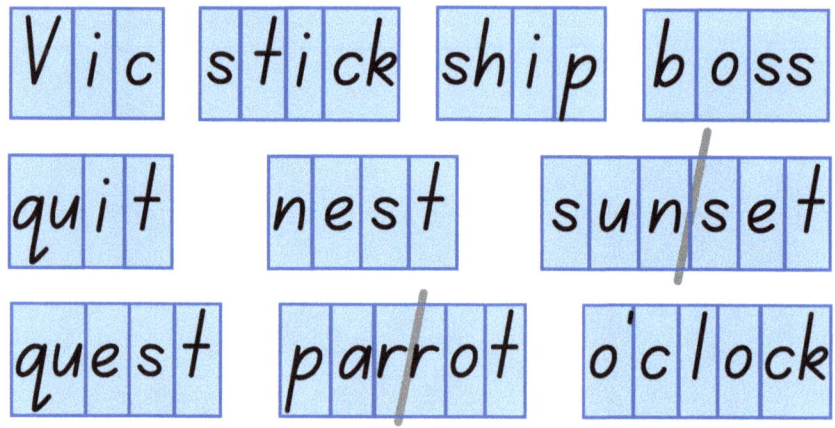

Vic stick ship boss
quit nest sunset
quest parrot o'clock

Practise tricky words

he she to do me we was
you no go they of are have
all t<u>all</u> c<u>all</u> her day for like

Gold

Set 4

Written by Kassi Gilmour

At sunset, a tall ship sets off on a quest.

Big Man is the boss.

He has a stick leg and a parrot.

He has a band of men to help.

Big Man has an old map. The map has an ✗, and this is the spot to dig for gold.

Big Man tells Vic to go up the nest to spot land.

"Scrub the deck!" he yells to his men.

At six o'clock the next day,
Vic spots land.

He tells his boss.

They dock the ship and jump off.

Then, they trek to the X spot from the map, but get stuck at a cliff.

"We will not quit!" Vic tells Big Man as he helps him up the cliff.

At the X, Big Man digs and digs and digs.

He hits a box.

A bolt locks the box shut.

Vic kicks the bolt off.

Gold and cash fill the box.

"We win!" Big Man tells Vic.

When they got back to the ship, they hid the gold.

"I have a map," Vic tells Big Man.

"Let's go!" calls Big Man.

Questions:

1. Who is on the ship?
2. Why does Big Man tell others what to do?
3. Who do you think Big Man trusts the most? Why?
4. Do you think Big Man and Vic will share the gold with the band of men? Why or why not?
5. Where do you think they will go now?

Trip to the Pond

Written by Kassi Gilmour

Practise the sounds

m s t a p i f c r o d h e n
g k ck u l ll ss ff b j w wh y
th sh v qu z zz x

Practise blending sounds

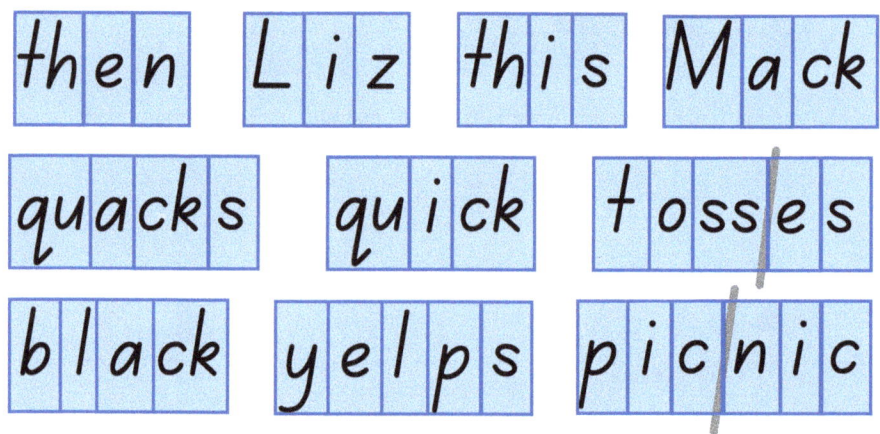

then Liz this Mack
quacks quick tosses
black yelps picnic

Practise tricky words

he she to do me we was you no
go they of are have all b<u>all</u> c<u>all</u>
sm<u>all</u> her day for like <u>likes</u>

Trip to the Pond

Set 4

WRITTEN BY KASSI GILMOUR

This is Mack. He is a dog and has a black back.

Mack likes to go to the pond.

"Mack, let us go to the pond,"
Liz tells Mack.

Mack yelps, "Yes!"

Mack and Liz go to the pond.

Mack is quick to trap a duck.

The duck quacks for help.
"No Mack! Stop it!" yells Liz.

Mack lets the duck go.

Then, Mack runs off and jumps on a picnic rug.

"No Mack! Get off!" calls Liz.

Liz gets her ball and tosses it.

Mack is quick to get it.

He yaps when he spots a small, soft dog.

Mack likes dogs.

Then, six kids run to pat Mack.

They like Mack.

Mack is hot, and hops into the pond for a swim.

"Mack! Let us go," Liz calls to her dog.

He has had a fun day at the pond.

Back at Liz's hut, Mack has a rest.

He likes his trips to the pond.

Questions:

1. Who owns Mack?
2. What things does Mack do at the pond?
3. Why do you think Mack likes to visit the pond?
4. Where do you like to visit? Why?

Play tricky word Tic Tac Toe

Players read each word correctly before placing their marker.

Aim: Be the first to get three in a row.

of	they	like
are	have	day
all	her	for

Vet

Written by Kassi Gilmour

Practise the sounds

m s t a p i f c r o d h e n
g k ck u l ll ss ff b j w wh y
th sh v qu z zz x

Practise blending sounds

vet   Max   this   van

then   tends   yaps

quick   fixes   helps

Practise tricky words

he she to in<u>to</u> do me we
was you no go they of are
have all c<u>all</u> her day for like

Vet

Set 4

Written by Kassi Gilmour

Pam's mum is a vet.

She helps sick dogs and cats.

Pam's mum has a vet van.

This van is quick, and can go to sick dogs and cats.

Pam's mum hops in the vet van.

The van is quick to get to Max.

Pam's mum picks Max up, and rests him on a soft bed in the van.

She fixes his leg.

Max will rest at the vet for the day.

Back at the vet, Pam's mum tends to Max.

Max is glad.

The next day, Max is up.
Pam's mum calls the man.

"Max is well and you can pick him up," the vet tells the man.

The man picks Max up.

He hugs his dog, and Max yaps.

Questions:

1. What job does Pam's mum do?
2. What happened at the pond?
3. Who did the man call and why?
4. How does the vet care for Max?
5. Where do you think Max will go now he is better?

Bugs

Written by Kassi Gilmour

Practise the sounds

m s t a p i f c r o d h e n
g k ck u l ll ss ff b j w wh y
th sh v qu z zz x

Practise blending sounds

| z | i | p | | Z | a | ck | | s | h | e | d | | b | u | zz |

| t | h | e | n | | s | h | r | u | b | s | | f | o | r | e | s | t |

| s | h | e | l | f | | f | u | ss | e | s | | s | t | r | o | ll | s |

Practise tricky words

he she to in<u>to</u> do me we was
you no go they of are have all
c<u>all</u> her day for like

Bugs

Set 4

Written by Kassi Gilmour

Zack and Dad have plans to go on a camp.

Zack is in the shed to help Dad pack.

Dad grabs a big, old box from the top shelf.

"This is the camp box," Dad tells Zack.

He kicks the lid off.

Dad jumps back as a big black bug was in the box.

"It is just a bug!" Zack tells Dad.

"I do not like bugs," Dad fusses.

Dad lifts up a big bag and tells Zack that it is the tent.

Zack sticks the tent in the truck.

Dad packs camp beds, rods and snacks too.

The next day, they go to the forest.

Lots of lush plants and shrubs fill the land.

Zack helps Dad set up the tent.

In go the camp beds and snacks.

"Zip up the tent!" Dad calls to Zack.

Dad grabs the rods. Then, they stroll to the dam to fish.

Next, they trek up a hill and swim in a pond.

At the end of the day, Zack and Dad hop into the tent.

Buzz, buzz, buzz!

All the bugs had got into the tent.

"Zack! You did not zip up the tent!" Dad yells.

Questions:

1. Where does Dad keep his camping gear?
2. Why do you think he uses his foot to take the lid off the camping box?
3. What activities do they do on camp?
4. Do you think they enjoyed the camping trip?

Fox

Written by Kassi Gilmour

Practise the sounds

m s t a p i f c r o d h e n
g k ck u l ll ss ff b j w wh y
th sh v qu z zz x

Practise blending sounds

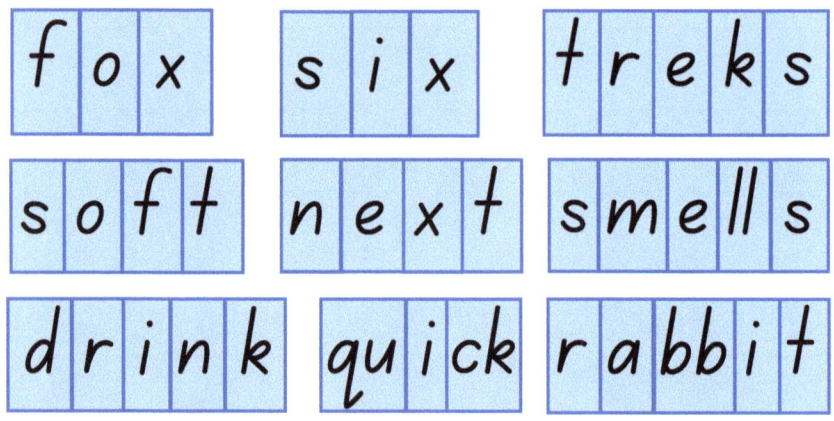

Practise tricky words

he she to in<u>to</u> do me we
was you no go they of are
have all her day for like

Fox

Set 4

Written by Kassi Gilmour

Six soft cubs rest on the rocks.

Mum fox sits next to her cubs.

Dad sets off to hunt.

He treks up a hill and smells rabbits.

They spot the fox, and are quick to dash into a log.

Next, he jogs to the pond and laps up a drink.

He spots a rabbit, and is quick to grab it.

Dad fox is in a rush to go back to his cubs.

The foxes like rabbit and are all glad.

Dad fox likes his six cubs.

Questions:

1. Who is in the fox family?
2. What do the cubs do?
3. Why does the mum fox stay near her cubs?
4. Why does the dad fox go hunting?
5. Have you ever seen a fox?

www.ingramcontent.com/pod-product-compliance
Lightning Source LLC
Chambersburg PA
CBHW040511110526
44587CB00045B/4260